Whispers from Silence

Amita Singh

BookLeaf
Publishing

India | USA | UK

Presentation by *BookLeaf Publishing*

Web: www.bookleafpub.com

E-mail: info@bookleafpub.com

ISBN: 9789363313484

First edition 2024

ACKNOWLEDGEMENT

I am grateful to all those who have contributed their presence, wisdom, and love.
I extend my appreciation to my friends Girija Acharya, Kuldeep Naik, Rakesh Singh and my daughter Anushka Singh. Your companionship has enriched both my writing and my life.

I am indebted to my Guru Akhilesh Joshi Sir and mentor Rangana Rupavi Choudhuri Mam, whose guidance has shaped my understanding of spirituality through which flows the poetry. Your teachings continue to inspire me to delve deeper into the realms of introspection and expression.

To the readers who embark on this poetic voyage, I express my gratitude for your curiosity, openness, and willingness to explore the realms of the heart and soul. May these poems resonate with your own journey of awakening and transformation.

Lastly with profound gratitude, I acknowledge the divine spark within us all, the source of creativity and inspiration that flows through every word and thought. May we continue to honor and nurture this sacred flame, illuminating our path towards greater understanding and connection.

PREFACE

Welcome to a journey through the soul, heart, and spirit. This collection of 71 poems dwells on themes of awakening, becoming whole, embracing spirituality, expressing gratitude, understanding cosmic rhythms, finding purpose, practicing self-acceptance, fostering self-love, and cherishing the present moment. These poems encourage you to let go of past regrets and future anxieties, and to immerse yourself in the vibrant beauty of the present.

In a world often characterized by haste and distraction, these poems invite you to pause and reflect on the profound truths that lie within and around us. They are an exploration of the human experience in its quest for meaning and connection with the greater universe. Each poem is a beacon of light, guiding you toward a deeper understanding of yourself and your place in the cosmos.

As you read through these poems, may you find inspiration, comfort, and a deeper connection to yourself and the world around you. Let them serve as a reminder that we are all part of a larger, beautiful whole, each with a unique role to play in the grand scheme of life. Go slow with the poems, embrace the journey with an open heart and mind, and may you discover the awakening, wholeness, and love that you seek.

TABLE OF CONTENTS

Here! My Karmas to mend............1

Stillness speaks............3

No Thing Nobody............5

Mind............ 6

Shift............ 8

Shadows............9

I am That Present............10

End, a new beginning............ 11

True Love🖤!............ 12

All is Worth🖤............ 13

Journey............ 14

Where "I" belongs............ 17

Let GO!............19

Who am I?............ 21

Path of Buddha............ 23

Becoming Shivai............ 24

Awakening............ 26

Becoming Whole............27

People pleaser............29

The Middle Path............ 31

Impermanence............ 32

Musings............ 34

I Believe!............ 35

Thank You!!............36

Feeling Deep...38

I am Awareness...39

I am still a Witness... 40

Cosmic Rhythm...41

Tiny wonders... 43

Alchemist..44

Move ON...45

Perceiver..46

Story... 48

As night falls..49

Passion..50

Down the memory lane.. 52

Missing parts.. 54

Wound...55

Purpose.. 56

I want myself... 57

Destiny..58

Prayer to parents...59

All happens for a reason.................................... 61

Lost.. 62

Tipping point.. 63

Oneness...65

Choose Myself...66

I Exist...67

Reminiscence..68

A love affair...70

The flute of Krishna..71

Grief Learnings......................................72

Every moment's a choice.........................74

Life ain't a race.................................. 76

Into the source.................................. 77

Self-love.................................... 79

Divergence.....................................81

Light.................................... 83

Running on circumference.............................. 85

Birth the new.................................. 86

Anything Real?.................................88

Not Good Enough.................................89

Self-Apology.................................... 90

Choice.....................................92

Time is Now.....................................94

Everyone Needs!.................................... 95

Here and Now!.................................... 96

I can be a mentor too.................................... 98

Neutral.................................... 100

Self-acceptance.................................... 101

How can I be free?.................................... 103

Here! My Karmas to mend

Being alive from infinity, no end
I am here for my Karmas to mend

I have climbed a thousand stairs
Sometimes I slide down to 100th there

As the calendar passes date
I don't know what will be my fate

As my emotions go on a roller coaster ride
I am sure to not be peace defied

Many times I tried and failed
But I have climbed up the emotional scale

With the thoughts, no more I fight
I just observe, to get them alright

I am light, I am love
I am just a peace-loving dove

With all when the Love I share
I become the species rarest, rare

My Being has just begun to shine
I am being blessed by love Divine

There is major shift in my attitude
Now I am more in Love and gratitude

Being alive from infinity no end
I am here for my karmas to mend

Stillness speaks

Life is but the experiences
Perceived through mind, its occurrences

The poor guy has gone through sin, agony, and
pain
Not once but again and again

The memories, ingrained of sorrow and rain
It refuses to trust the existence of sunshine again

So much that it feels victimized
To change the pattern, it needs to be customized

To erase the habit-pattern of pain
Mind has to learn to make memories again

This time the focus has to be sky, not clouds
It needs to change to stillness from doubts

Because what you see is what you get
You cannot remain dry by perceiving wet

THAT (almighty) can be experienced through
body and Mind
Not until, you start to perceive the Divine

It must evolve from contraction (doubt, anger,
frustration, ..) to expanse
To experience 'That', experience enhance
(vastness, unlimited, completeness, fulfillment,
divinity)

In the end, it's all a mind game
Then why not involve where you win not shame

In your Heart (expanse) when the attention
(Mind) sits
That is when, the stillness speaks.
That is when the stillness speaks!!

No Thing Nobody

There is nothing, nobody
    yet No Thing exists
There is nothing, nobody
    yet It just IS
There is nothing, nobody
    yet 'I' exists
There is nothing, nobody
    the time is Here and NOW
There is nothing, nobody
    yet love persists
There is nothing, nobody
    And no feelings now

There is nothing, nobody
    In silence exists no shape
It's Zero, nowhere to go
    Nothing to Be
Open the eyes and see
    It's just space
It's just space
    It is vast, Infinite
Limitless, just like the sky
    It's never born, nor does it die

Mind

The mind has no attribute of its own
It just projects, what you judge, dislike, disown

Your relations are your mind's reflection
Seeking to drop judgement and choose love and
affection

It reflects even more, the more you try to hide
The more of same situation comes your way, the
more you push aside

There is a part of you in me
And part of me in you

Some accepted, some unacceptable trait
On each other, we reflect

The unacceptable ones are cause of concern
To us, it pushes apart and run

And until the unacceptable remains
There is heartache and pain

Until You explore yourself, all your traits you
find

No matter how much you run away, you attract
again a similar kind

Once you have accepted you
With nothing left or due

The situation now makes a shift
As you change the people change, remains no
more a rift

All you need to do here is offer yourself your
help
Accept all unacceptable, completely all yourself

The purpose is to accept oneself completely in
your heart
Journey is to become whole, not remain in parts

The acceptance that you seek from world when
it comes within
Here is joy of freedom and love, No forgiveness,
no sin

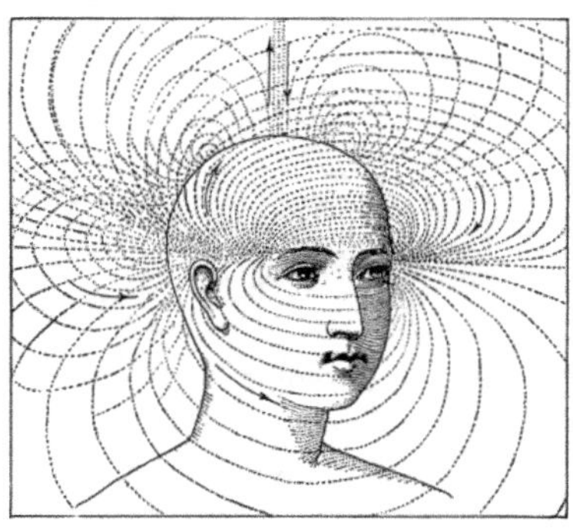

Shift

Now there is shift from worry to care
There is change from fear to 'All is fair'
It is not about Doing, it's just about Being there

Set them free from expectations, to love and accept
All Being's full of Love, joy, and share

Let's create a space of peace and hope
And let's drop off all the Despair

Let all go, let all just Fly
Be open to all, just like the vast Sky

Just not shower Any with Advice
Of what is vicious and vice

Allow them to just stumble and fall
Just BE when they need your presence at all

Shadows

There is Sage in me,
Yet there is also Rage.

There is Seeker in me,
Yet there is also a cheater.

There is motivator in me,
So also a manipulator.

There is fear in me,
So also some tears.

There is Love,
So also some lust

Ready here and now,
to accept all that I must

It is just the time to evolve,
let all of me die, dissolve all pain

Let just That remain
Life then would be full of meaning,
Not in vain

I am That Present

My poems are reflections of my mind
Now I choose to leave the past behind
Not travel to the future as it is unseen
Just be present and enjoy the Being

Getting aware of every choice and breathe
Allow pain to take time and recede
It's time to embrace joy and peace
Just let go off all the dis-ease

Allow myself to expand and explore
Become the ocean as well, the shore
No more cramping in mind's Tunnel
Set completely free to accept all miracle

I see myself as *I am That
Present* ♥ all around
Fulfilled in delight and complete
I am all allowing and profound

End, a new beginning

A journey has come to an end
And a new one just begun
Hold on, just breathe
No longer need to run

What all seek, it's always HERE
Just let go off all guilt, anguish, and fear
Feel the love, and feel the Divine
It's all in you, dark night, or sunshine

It's HERE where choices need to be made
To drop all pain, the foundation of Joy to be laid
Open your wings, get ready to fly.
Become love and explore the sky

True Love!

For despite what some people say,
Love is not only a sweet feeling bound to come
and go away.
When true love rises in Self, it just continues to
stay.

With every breath, it nourishes the soul,
With every moment it makes you whole.

The more it grows, you get silent and still
Not one desire left, but follow God's Will

There's always a secret joy
Freedom from, mind's lament and cry.

The more it grows, the more it's deep
Makes you ready for a Divine leap

Life ain't about pass by and go
It is more about loving oneself and grow

All is Worth 🖤

The question remains is
Who am I
No identity seems to identify

When birds chirp my heart seems to bounce
All it wants is to announce

I love this world and the world loves me
The wisdom takes over, says Just BE

The stillness speaks, this needs no Identity
All that is needed is already here
The being squeaks in joy, no trace of fear

Lose all identity and Die before death
For expansion and space, all is worth 🖤

Journey…

It all began a while ago
When I was raw, not able to let go

I crumbled, I gathered, I stood up from fall
All kept me going was a Divine call

While I put all myself, at stake
It was a journey of make and break

All the way, I seeked was acceptance somehow
I could not understand what's self-love

The churning brought all emotions to surface
I couldn't hide my slimy face

The journey was tough and so many left
Many sleepless nights, on the pillow I wept

I broke into pieces and thought had to stop
Yet kept going with just a little hope

I was naive to understand the game
Yet stood there to embrace all that came

The journey into the unknown, not knowing
much myself
Blessed by Gurus who held up and helped

The pain now sent shivers down my spine
All that I knew was my being was to shine

Suddenly one day at the dawn outbreak
I started to quake, shiver and shake

The rush of energy moved up my spine
Suddenly everything felt so very Divine

My mind wavered, said I am about to die
It rose again in a whining cry

My heart went still and expansion I felt
I could witness my ego melt

The shine of the Divine is what I could see
I now heard don't resist, "Just BE"

Untwining third eye, one breath - one voice
'I'he mind dissolved, in no noise

All prevailing silence yet thousand bells ring
My heart flooded with light, radiates to sing

It is worth to allow and let the ego die
And awaken to the truth of Who am I

It's freedom from bondage, suffering and cry
Descending to light with love and joy

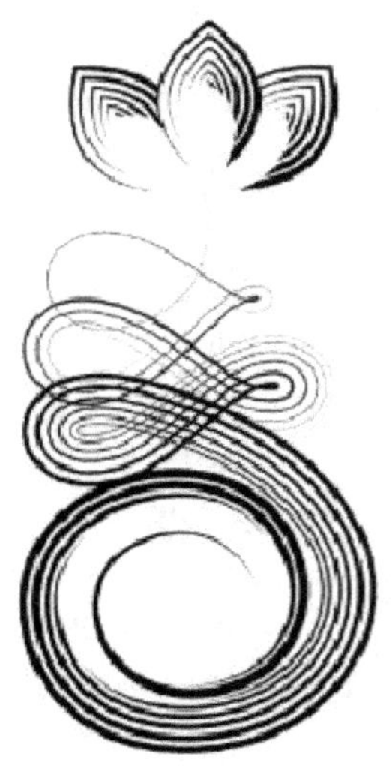

Where "I" belongs

I was afraid of Silence,
Realized that is where 'I' belongs
There arises poetry
And there arises the songs

The Mind sinks in Heart Divine
With bubbles of light, the heart shines
In every cell this love is felt
The Ego now, slowly melts

Every step there is a test
Mind that's left does not rest
It arises and shows
The face that you fake
Shows that your existence is Namesake

Do not get caught in this drama of Mind
Be the Witness, let awareness shine
That's how "i" of Ego melts
And the Soul light of "I" is felt

When you know the source of Mind
You have the power of Divine
As now in awareness the feelings you choose
In Mind thoughts, you do not let loose

Slowly now, every thought dissolves
There is emptiness, the Soul evolves
It takes over the control from Mind
In this awareness, the light shines

Every memory of past now erased
No worry of future, no need to chase
All the drama just comes to an end
All the karmas are set to mend

Where 'No thing' remains
"I" is an 'Infinite Hole'
This 'No thing' is Permanent
And disappears ALL

("i" is Ego, "I" is Soul)

Let GO!

Don't be a person who holds it too tight
Allow yourself to release it when it's no longer
right
Don't wait for the blisters, and your heart and
fingers to ache
Coz holding on is not worth the pain, that it
takes

Release the part of you, that slowly you had
become
Remember that it's not you, as it's making you
numb
Drop the ones who felt so dear
As holding on is inducing fear

Convince your heart, some things are not meant
to be long
It arrived to teach a lesson, it's time to move on
Not cling to people who don't make you smile
Don't waste your energy, it's not worthwhile

Leave some things that you are fighting for
It's not worth the cost
As everything you lose
Was eventually to be lost

Fight your little battle and fight it for yourself
When it gets difficult alone, just seek someone's
help
Love yourself, the best you can
It's the biggest lesson of the Divine plan

Seek nothing outside of you
Rest will treat yourself, just the way you
                    Simply DO..

Who am I?

A profound silence so deep within
As subtle as the depth of Ocean
I ain't the voice in the head, but the one who
observes the voice
An awareness just before the thought
A space where thoughts begin

I ain't the body, I ain't the mind
I simply am Divine
I am life, I am love
Complete in self, pure profound
In everything and All, I can be found

Get going, get aware of yourself
It's all within, just seek its help
Get aware of your soul's voice
The mind, aloud it chatters and speaks
The soul, it's soft and silently squeaks

It's not the self, to identify with forms
Physical, thoughts or emotional norms
This results in unconnected forgetfulness, an
original sin
From intrinsic oneness, source which exists
within

When delusion of separateness is root and
governs
Manifests misery, haywire life runs
Need is to train and restructure the mind
To stop creating evil reality and experience
Divine

Path of Buddha

Walking the path of Truth, is the work of bold
It takes courage to leave the path, age old
When Buddha is born, troubles unfold
It begins a competition unknown, untold

All target him for the wisdom he hath
Jealous of his boldness to take the new path
Their ego is bent, but knowledge withholds
Frightened still, to get out of safety mold

The Buddha turns to ashes as ego burns
Crowds target him, taking turns
He is left all alone, in the search of Tao
That doesn't waver the bold one's vow

He keeps walking, with a prayer
When there is creation, must be a creator there
Until the drop meets the ocean within
Experiences are milestones, not a Win

The journey continues until lessons learnt
Every bit of "i" is totally burnt
The Ego Mind dissolves in Self
Buddha stands now, for others' help

Becoming Shivai

Bhagirath had a special prayer
A unique and rarest of rare
Asked how he can set himself free
From life and death misery
Free his ancestors and lineage as well
Could someone guide and tell

He got his reply
"Get Ganges on earth from sky"
But to hold the pressure of Ganges
He would need to please Shivai
Meditation, he began then
With penance and pain

He meditated for a long age
Earned recognition as a sage
Illuminated with enormous light
Ego in him, not left slight
The cosmic Ganges descended from sky
As he himself became Shivai

The cosmic Ganga has the power that heals
From all past emotions and feels
The emotions and feeling is where the Karmas
hold
To walk this path is the task of bold

All one needs is, to awaken to self
And Ganges mother, flows down for help

The Ganga thus in physical form
Is worshiped, not just out of norm
She has supreme powers to heal
Making lives full of zeal
And to become the creator of one's own destiny
Awakening the Shivai within, is the deal

Awakening

On the ground, as I lie
I feel myself as an infinite boundless sky
The essence of creation I now feel
The mind has gone, silent and still

I see everything just vanish in the air
The plant, the trees, the sun nothing's there
I glide through the dark tunnel of mind
And merge on another side with light Divine

Now as my life, I recall
I see the mind is the creator of all
From tiny ants to the deepest ocean
Exists only in mind's perception

It's Now to find the source of mind
Go beyond the light, said guidance Divine
As I venture ahead of light
There is "NO thing" at all in sight

All I see is formless me
As vast and deep as the sky and sea
The mind has now stopped to wander
In the source, it has surrendered

Becoming Whole

This eve feels special today
I lay in grass so green
Gazing infinite sky so vast
I witness, what I had never seen

Staring at the endless sky
It's the sky or I went still
My heart expanding in joy so deep
Gratitude in all, I feel

Awake early morning the next day
To witness a Divine kiss
The orange sun when touched the sky
An experience, not to miss

The sky melted; the sun stripped in layers
Pulled I felt, in a funnel
Tingling, twirling, to open knots between the
brows
I realized, I was in a mind tunnel

Down the path, I witnessed all my lives
In the dark, unknown- feeling the fear
A voice I heard to not resist
As liberation was just near

I surrendered every bit of me
Witnessing where I was being lead
Reached the other side of the tunnel
To witness a never seen light instead

Into the light, when myself merged
There was peace, and bliss
No beginning no end
O! Nothing exists, yet ALL Just IS

Go beyond, said the voice so I traveled beyond
It was a space so still and calm
"i" dissolved in Nothingness
Hearing a silent Psalm

All "I AM", was just in Mind
And it dissolved in Heart
All stories came to an end
Becoming whole, from remains and parts!!

People pleaser

I was born of pure love,
The essence of love Divine
The life happened on the earth
Divided in yours and mine

All that I did was seldom my choice
I saw my world through others' eyes
O what I cook, what do I wear
Born out of fear, not love and care

My heart felt weak and my mind strong
Always ready to prove where I went wrong
Came a time no matter what I did
Just had to face the people rigid

My quest for love felt above the sky
The storm in my heart was roaring high
All that I did was to seek love
I suppressed myself into a timid dove

I felt my survival was at stake
Chose to remove my natural and go fake
All I did, was people please
While ME within was not at ease

I knew by now, something's not right
I am fighting myself, with all my might
And what I gained in this quest
Was diseased heart, highly unrest

The quest again, began from the Start
It was now, within my heart
When my mind went still, it's then I found
I killed myself to please around

Forgiveness to myself was the Call
THIS happened as I allowed it All
All that I did was seldom my choice
I saw my world with others' eyes

This moment of grief was a Powerful shift
It's time to let go and receive a new gift
With open arms I stared at the sky
So much peaceful and vast was I

The heart expanded to claim in all
I was both, the big and small
Vanished all past, dissolved the pain
In the beauty of the moment Nothing remained

To forgive was to set a prisoner free
I knew by now; the prisoner was me
All the love I seek was always in me
To feel it all, I choose to remain Free

The Middle Path

I see now when the stories end
There is no desire left to repair or mend
The mind stops to oscillate in doer ship quiz
A stillness prevails in all that is

An extreme silence, after gongs-bells stop
All needs fade to yield the desired crop
With every story now, dies little ego
No mercy, no forgiveness, no need to let go

All that exists is Divine grace
Full of love, compassion, and space
The mind just skids and settles in NOW
Free from why, where, what and how

The chapter now dissolves and closes
Body shakes, quivers as memory disposes
We live together a collective story
As One evolves, the others too are set free

Here there is no loss or gain
Just freedom from pleasure and pain
Into nothingness, settles the heart
Neutral is natural, Buddha's middle path.

Impermanence

It was yet another
A night of grief and pain
I tried my best to get over it
But all efforts in vain

I just kept gazing at the sky
The little that I could see
So much pain all over the world
How could there peace be

Trauma, anger, revenge and grief
Turmoil of emotions within
So much dirt, so much stink
I felt like a garbage bin

Pain in that moment was so high
The Universe felt in grief
I was the cause of all this in the world
Can my death bring them relief?

I saw myself in the ocean deep
There was no breathing space
I blamed myself for everything
And how I was just a disgrace

I didn't know when I was swallowed by sleep
The grief still an inseparable part
In that moment I witnessed the magic
When light emerged from my heart

All cells illuminated
It was a dance of joy
The Heart felt expansive
Now clearer looked the sky

A voice spoke within myself
You are not the happenings, just remain as the
sky
Let emotions express themselves,
Like the weather passing by

Just witness it all, and drift in none
And neutral when you remain
Soon you see, you will be out
Of the matrix of pleasure and pain

Musings

Some fall in love with the cold
Some with the heat
Yet all crave to come back to their own
Comfortable sheet
Is it all a momentary Myth?

Loving, liking and connect
with someone is a natural feat
All this happens when wavelengths meet
Then hating, dis-liking and dis-connect
Also is a natural feat
And happens when wavelengths refuse to meet

Is unconditional love a myth?
Or it just means, without any (un)conditions
In every situation, just fit

I Believe!

Time stands still
      Beauty in all I feel
As I just hold my breath
      Feeling my fears fade
Working on self from start
      Now I found home in my heart
I feel, I am enough
      No longer it needs to be tough
It's all just Love, love and love
I believe!!

Tears flow down my eyes
      Each drop sparkles in joy
My being is about to shine
      With the light of the Divine
The voice within is clear
      Liberation is just near
I believe!!

Thank You!!

Thank you for the Rains
   that make me wet
Thank you for the storm
   that made me firm
Thank you for the times,
   I bore the harm

Thank you for the air,
   that I breathe
Thank you for
   the songs in me
Thank you for the times,
   I couldn't see

Thank you for the plunge
   and dive
Thank you for moments,
   I am alive
That you for the Love,
   that heals
Thank you for the Grace,
   that feels

Thank you for the sun
   that shines
Thank you for the presence,

Divine
Thank you for the moonlit
        sky
Thank you for the energy;
        high

Thank you for one heart
        that beats in Infinite
Thank you for one breath
        in each
Thank you for the rise
        and high
Thank you for seat
        in the lap of Thy
Thank You!!

Feeling Deep..

Every single breath is felt
Every identity is set to melt
Every illusion must now dissolve
The Time now has come to evolve

Every drama is to end
Every karma is to mend
Every doubt must come to rest
Trust that all happens for the Best

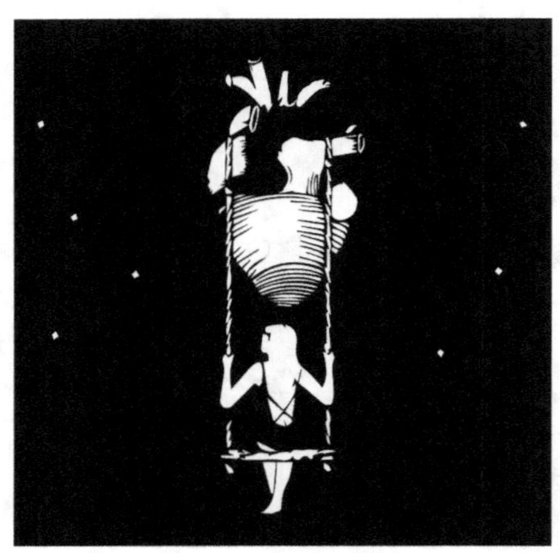

I am Awareness

I am awareness
I am present every moment
I do not judge any person or event

I am awareness
Infinite and vast as Skies
In my presence, life simplifies

I am awareness
Now and Here the Ego dissolves
Just as then, the Truth starts to evolve

I am awareness
I Exist from time begin to infinity
As deep as the ocean, through the mountains I
see

I am awareness
In my light, nothing is a mystery
Here I show, the purpose of life is to "Just BE"

I am still a Witness

As I feel completely complete
I become Nothing and yet the source
I am still a witness

All just creating through me
All just culminating in me
I am still a witness

Thousand bells ring
The cells disintegrate and recreate
I am still a witness

Profound Silence and peace prevails
All the contracts and carnage ends
I am still a witness

Cosmic Rhythm

This is the space of Love and Joy
Beyond judgement, open your heart to cry
Sing all the songs that you never sung
No matter how old or young
You are welcome here!

Just let them go
Go with the flow
Dance in the rain
And sing in the pain
You are welcome here!

Stand again after every fall
Love yourself, just love it all
There is no wait, for the Divine call
All you seek is already here
You are welcome here!

Soon there is an end to the pain
Going beyond the loss and gain
Embracing all insanity and sane
I am welcome here!

Life is all about the choice
Accept all, vicious and vice
Discover yourself and rejoice
Be the welcome here!

Tiny wonders

Tiny little droplets that we call tears
Are just not expressions of sorrow and fear
It's the wrong definition we gave
It can express anything, it's so naïve
It's ok to cry when overwhelmed with joy
It's courageous to express, not suppress in self

Are not women more natural I sometimes think
As tears flow down at the sight of a lovely wink
It's alright as much for a man to cry
As he too is human, not a robotic try
Nature didn't discriminate between woman and
man
It has given both equal tear glands

Hold it not back, let every droplet flow
With every little droplet let love and compassion
grow
Tears can express the unheard
It is more powerful than unuttered words

Dear wonderful mothers do teach your Child,
It's ok to cry
It's ok to express through tears
May it be pain or joy

Alchemist

War is about to end
Peace in place, all about to mend

We all are born with certain alchemy
It's in you, so also in me.

All the need is to drop the thinking mind
And enter the kingdom Divine

No fear of past, no future worry
Walk beyond the Mind story

Shed the past patterns of sadness, trauma and lie
Fill oneself with fulfillment and joy

As you always get, what you seek
Then seek the strength, why seek weak

We have the power to create our destiny
Isn't it a serious alchemy?

Move ON

Moving on in life, letting it go
Can be too much of a pain
Just until you realize
Holding me on is causing an energy drain

Hold on takes much space in Mind
It refrains you from reaching Divine
To hold on means no forgiveness yet
No forgiveness means, there is still some regret

This regret takes away your peace
A piece of you remains in piece
What's meant to be yours
You are bound to get
All it needs is patience and wait

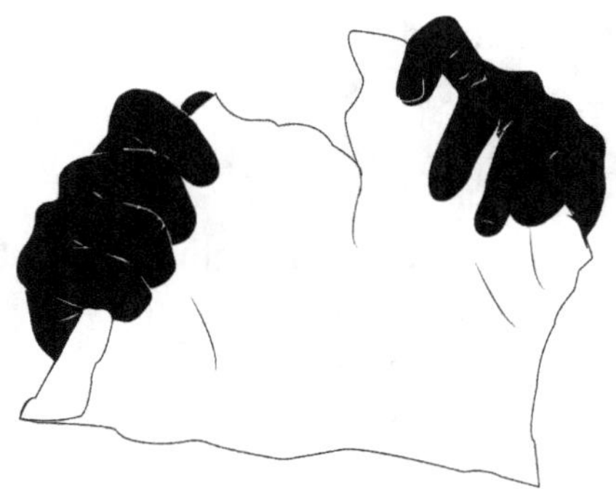

Perceiver

It does matter how things feel.
Not gauge feelings for right and wrong
They are here as the moment's truth
Have come to express the inner song

There is silent inner spaciousness
That is more clear
much more significant
to be aware of, than feelings mere

Feelings, moods and thoughts
Are perceived to come and go in a bit
Identify with them to perceive
The tendencies or habit

Somehow, the one who perceives
is most overlooked
It's always silent and still
Never to be shook

The conscious that perceives, the momentary
has the power to ignore.
It is ever untouched and
unchangingly present in the Core

Your guide is an anchor
to walk the lonely path
You alone can confirm the truth
When it's felt in your heart

Story

It took some time to pen my story
From feeling lost to Satori
There were step-ups, fall and rise
Many layers of self-disguise

So many identities but not one real
Images of me, all surreal
There was no hope, no vision of self
All I seeked was approval and help

Many people crossed my path
Some blissful, some judgmental in heart
Oh god, so much is my effect!
Whole world is just, what I reflect

In order to build my world Divine
I have to work on clearing my mind
The layers of Mind one by one peeled
Slowly within I felt, I healed

As night falls

Every night when I am in bed
My heart fills up with light
Every cell illuminates with joy
My being shines up so bright

My ears hear the ocean waves
The stillness fills up so deep
Body quivers in jerks and chills
Mind takes up a leap

The needs dissolve
And desires melt
I dissolve in me
No separation is felt

Nothing seems too far
What I seek is already here
My true love self
No anger, resentment, drama or fear

Passion

My passion is
        to fly high
Take a leap to touch the sky

My passion is
        to roar like the sea,
And I want to humm like a bee

My passion is
        to set myself free,
to find myself in all of Me

My passion is
        to live to fullest
until my last breath when I remain in rest

My passion is
        to settle in me,
And open my arms to embrace all of Thee

My passion is
        to burn that "i"
That separates me from the existence of Thy

My passion is
        to clean the Mind's slate,
Where I am no more governed by fate

My passion is
        to liberate my shadows unheard
All along I felt were absurd

My passion is
        to heal my past
And contribute in healing the present that lasts

My passion is
        to forgive and feel
The freedom of joy, happiness and zeal

My passion is
        to explore the love I am
Freedom from hatred, guilt and shame

All along I abused myself
        Never did I seek for help
My passion now is to love that abuser in me, that
is how it can be set free

Down the memory lane

Looking down the memory lane, I find myself
burnt in pain
I never felt loved, supported and cared
No matter how well in life, I faired
My parents blessed me with physical fortunes
Unaware of emotions in my heart, a feeling of
sand dunes

Feeling trapped in body shelf
I had lost the trust in Self
No more love for myself I felt
Life became a hell to be dealt

I saw myself collapse in a bit
By pain of lifetimes, I had got hit
My relationship with myself went to worst
To seek love from all, I put them first
I felt insignificant and used by all
Really tiny and utterly small

I lost myself in willowed lane
No hope to find myself again
All bits and pieces, I picked myself
Shouted loud now seeking help
Some hands stood by to hold, let me not fall
All along I masked, being tall

Until I realized it's all my fault
To check my thoughts, I took a halt
The outside mess that I could see,
Was actually my inner reality
In acceptance to all I felt myself shine
It's no more mess, it was all mine

Giving me power to hold and own
I now knew outer world, is inner one's clone
I started to sweep the dirt in sight
With all the power, and all my might

With every breath, awareness I built
Experienced the mind sway on every bend and
tilt
Soon mind pendulum came to a halt
I felt all's well and nothing's at fault

I started to put right thoughts in place
Accepting the old with full embrace
Thinking right and create new feel
Has got me here, and now I am healed

Missing parts

Working relentlessly on myself
I found the missing parts of me
The parts that I hadn't loved
The parts that never felt enough

The parts that wanted to people please
The parts that were not at ease
The parts that wanted to earn appreciation
Going to the levels of non acceptance

The parts that I hated in me
No good in myself I would see
Feeling worthless was another shell
Self-doubt, fears is where I dwelt

Accept the unacceptable said the Grace
Allowed it all in an embrace
I found nothing was missing in me
A voice whispered and said "Just Be"

Wound

There is a wound, in my heart
And it is still alive
Don't know what is remaining though
I am ready to take a dive

I feel some pain in my heart
The pain is of grief
It's the feeling of abandonment
Feels like fallen leaf

I feel a pressure within my throat
Wanting to cry out loud
Feel a constant pull in liver
Could someone help me shout

Weird sensations
Pins and poky feel
A silent cry goes out to sky
Can someone help me heal?

Purpose

The whole journey is to get the Mind to Still
Wandering from ages in realms and fields

Progress from Body, Mind to Soul
Dropping all identities and roles

Peel layer by layer to reach the core
Until there is almighty, nothing more

I am all prevailing consciousness
Traveling through lifetimes

The journey is not of body
The journey is of mind

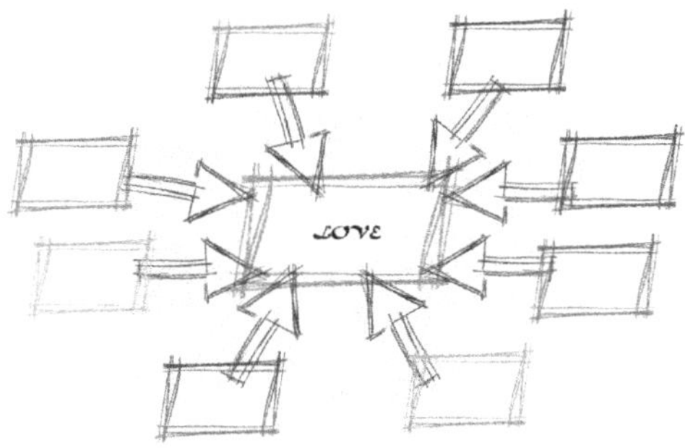

I want myself

Feeling unloved, unwanted from ages ago
I knew not whom to ask, where to go

Pain so deep, would make me cry
left me no choice but to die

Into nowhere my life sailed
attempt of suicide, that too failed

In pursuit to earn some love
I became the best over and above

Yet the wait never came to an end
My life's reality refused to mend

I choose now to want myself
Close all unloved, unwanted on shelf

I love myself and all of me
From time begin to infinity

Hear a whisper in my ears
And I hear it so clear

Extending arms, its calling out
I want you, I want you all my dear!

Destiny

I feel I belong here
But nothing belongs to me

What I have or what I get
Is just what's the destiny

Some I may get, some I may not
It's all a part of the Divine plot

Life presents with constant choice
Consequences of same we are to rejoice

Prayer to parents

Oh my dear parents, who all are here
Be there with your kids in darkness and tears
Just don't be a provider and perform your task
Be there in times of trauma, disconnects and
fears

Let your child welcome all the dark
Let them cherish every bit of feelings, allow
them express but not balk
For every feeling they hide, a part of themselves
they reject
And grow into a human feeling unloved and
disconnect

Oh my dear parents, what your dear children
really seek
Is the emotional connect and love in times when
they are weak
Hold their hands and let them know
You are ALL there, down the dark tunnel or
mountain peak

For in times when they reject themselves, your
acceptance will flourish
They learn to accept themselves, hold on and
cherish

Oh my dear parents, love every bit of your child
Strong, shallow, timid or mild

When you love them for their presence and
being
They start to accept all of them, everything
All acceptance leads to Love, Gratitude and
Grace
They open to infinite space and Divine embrace

All happens for a reason

All that happens is for a reason
As crops grow with the change of seasons

All that you have, on your plate
Was through your ask, soon or late

What we see now, is a small window frame
However, it's the result of a lifetime's game

The beliefs that we carry define the course of
life
Good, bad, ugly, easy or full of strife

Every thought we create changes in life's flow
Observe, rethink, replace, just go a little slow

Soon you will definitely conquer your mind
That's when your Divinity will start to shine

Lost

Oh, sometimes I feel so lost
Not knowing what am I searching for
Don't know, when this search began
Don't know, I have reached how far

All I feel is away from home
Paths unknown
Where to go or where to come
All I feel is a blank sky

I keep drifting between solitude and lonely
And silence sometimes makes me still
Enough of pain and drama I've seen
To set myself free is my only will

Tipping point

Not until the tipping point is reached
No opportunity to awaken is seized

Life sets alarms, creating situations
One is still busy in Mind's palace, illusion

The illusion tunnel, has more and more grooves
The deeper one gets stuck, it's difficult to move

Life suffocates, it's a struggle to breathe
For every bit of oxygen, One starts to plead

It feels like a vacuum, all seems so dull
Life makes one look at, what's void and null

Life throws back to one's own face
The parts and paths, left untraced

One Is forced to walk these paths
Collect and gather all the broken parts

The pain is deep, the suffering still a choice
One can hear, One's own chatters and noise

Journey begins to train-untrain the mind
Forgive oneself and remain kind

Process to learn unlearn relearn begins
Facing oneself, the good and sins

Now in this moment, tipping point is reached
The opportunity to awaken is now seized

Oneness

The Journey is about to end, collecting pieces
here and there
Who Am I, is what I asked and found myself
everywhere

It's all in Mind, came the voice
Life's a game of options and choice

The wiser you get, the choices get better
Each step empowers, no repents later

Creating emotions or remain unwavered still
Has become a choice of will

No more guilt, no more shame
No more hurt, and no other to blame

Choose Myself

I allow myself
       to break the walls and build the bridge
To meet myself on the other side
I want myself, no more to hide

Into the universe, all through my heart
I allow myself to shine my light
It's come to me, also everyone's right

I embrace myself, just all of me
The unfortunate, unwanted, unloved and ugly

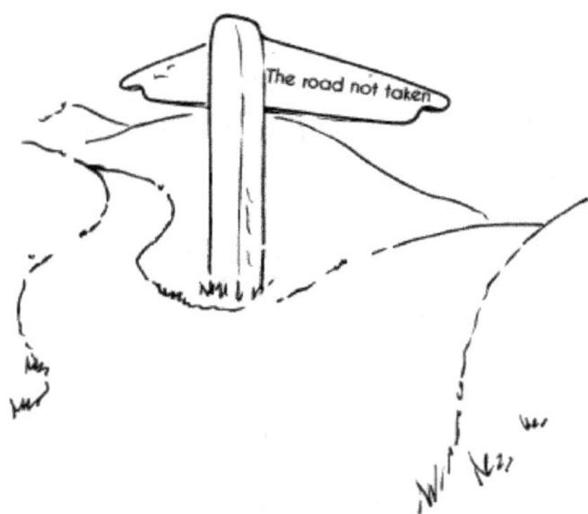

I Exist

In the silence of this space
Infinite and Small

I exist into Existence
Nothing and All

Watching my body dissolve and melt
All the love and bliss being felt

I am the Universe and Universe is in me
How vast and expansive can I be

The illusions now, are dissolved
I am the evolution and evolved

Reminiscence

I see myself suffocating in fire ablaze
Gasping for breath
Watching life fade
In fire and smoke
Watching this body die
The muscles melt in furnace
I hear myself howl and cry

This isn't the way to die
This isn't the way to die
Bewildered, I ask for help
My muscles now melting into pulp
Every breath though is becoming deep
What did I sow, for this to reap?

Now I gasp even deeper for breath
Watching myself nearing death
I see my life's journey behind
Brave, compassionate, cruel or kind

It was all for others' ease
All I did was people please
I needed to learn was to trust my gut
Allow trust in Divine, no if no but

And act through truth, not people please
Put myself first with love and ease
Allow this love to flow through all
Become the instrument for Divine call

As I die now,
I see, it's not an end
I will be coming back for my karmas to mend
There is peace now, with last breath to die
No one has gone alive from this world, neither
did I

A love affair

A love affair of me,
with ME
I no more please the people, to BE

I choose myself first, over anybody
No it's not ego, it's love for myself
If not me for ME then who else will help
Yes, I choose my own embrace
With all the love, care and grace

Through all the pleasure and pain
Through all the losses and gain
I dare to dream and make it true
My life! I choose to live on my view

A love affair of me,
with ME
I no more please the people, to BE
I choose myself first, over anybody

The flute of Krishna

The ancient flute of Krishna
Has 7 holes
Is it just a coincidence
Or there is a symbolic role?

I venture deep into the ocean
The more I question my Mind
I feel here,
there is definitely a purpose Divine

It's to rise from Mooladhar to Sahasrara
Using the rhythmic breath
Creating own music
Expand widespread

For the music to play
And then I think, ahh, it's hallow
So to reach Devine, one has to get empty of
thoughts
Deep or shallow

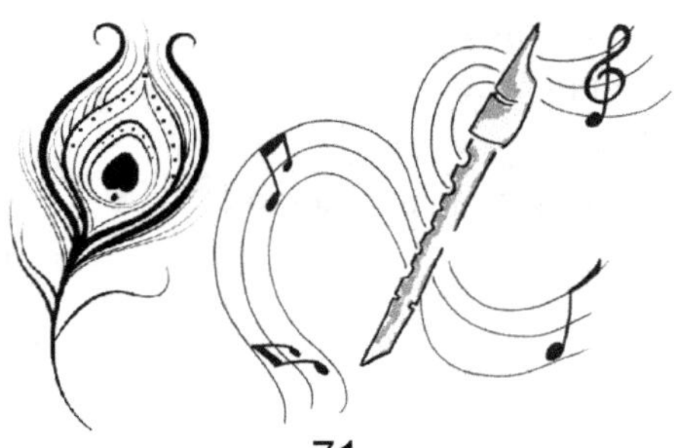

Grief Learnings

When my heart felt heavy
Laden with grief
The sky would cry
The earth would weep

In the ocean of sorrow
Not getting any help
In the quest to survive
I lost myself

The pain would flow
In every little cell
Life became a burden
As deep as hell

All did I notice
Was sorrow and pain
Separation and abandonment
A quest to reach home again

Just then I noticed
It's all in my mind
The intention now set
Being compassionate and kind

What I didn't get from others
Was missing in me
Through my shadows
I began to see

The will so strong
For the love to seek
Gave the strength
Now no more weak

All I need to change
Is just me, the world ain't my responsibility
Soon the sky felt vast
The earth in bliss
Life seemed easy
With a Divine kiss

Every moment's a choice

Every moment gives a choice
To live from memory
Or make new history
To act from known realm
Or from unknown mystery

All that is past
Is appearance in time and space
To create something new
All old must erase

Nothing stable here
All is in flow
To recognize the core
Just go a little slow

See how life springs from Nothing
And is always so fresh
Like writing on water
It leaves no trace

No one can step into the same waters twice
The river is always in flow
How can you be free
When you act out of memories, just from what
you know

The seed that grows with water, sun and love
Is creator in creation
Break it open to find
It's empty, nothing-none

See all emerge from emptiness
Nothingness is the source
You must be empty yourself
To experience the dance of conscious

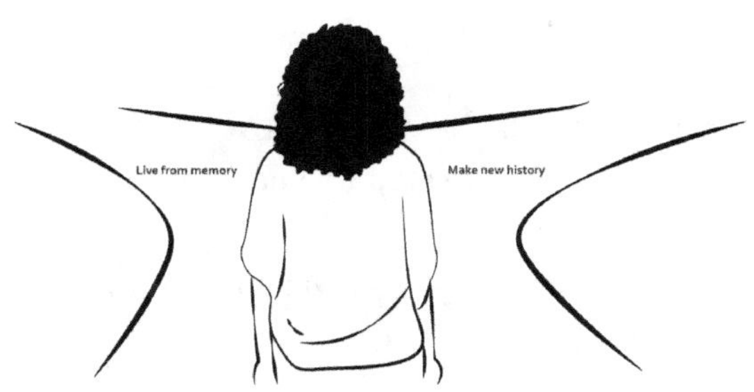

Life ain't a race

So many times I lose the track
Four steps up and two steps back

So many times I miss the pace
Just to realize life isn't a race

So many times I happen to say
It's life and it's happening this way

It's how the lessons, it teaches
To and fro before one reaches

Worth my love is for you to know
Not allow anyone to step up and show

When time comes by, you wake up to shine
Until then just wait for the sign

Into the source

One day it so happened
Nor there was an observer and neither I
All became silent and still
Like the midnight sky

The stars still were shining
Till all vanished into a hole
Returning all to dust
Yet remaining whole

All that I was listening to
Was the thumping of my heart
One breath of one creation
Inclusive all, not apart

I found myself in another realm
Nothing at all to see
I existed in existence
And existence was in me

The more I drifted into it
The stillness went more strong
The attention drifted into my heart
Said here's where I belong

The calmness of the silence
Went so much into deep
Every cell busted in joy
Not leaving any to weep

Self-love

Here, we are raised to people please
Full of guilt, apathy and hate
Self-love, often feels selfish
A struggle to maintain peace

Living in an era of self-love revolution
The trouble is to practice
Knowing not the feelings - emotions,
the fundamental foundation

The essence of who we are
Our needs, identifications
It's about being true to oneself
Beyond any judgement or assumptions

Learning to celebrate the beauty within
Reaching out first to one's own help
It no more feels like a trap
No more hiding behind the shelf

It's knowing what's good for you
No tolerance for treatment as crap
No preventing yourself from good
Choice gets easy, flip or swap

The saboteur behavior goes away
No destructions, no more rude
It is taking self-ownership
Accepting self the way one should

Time to set the things right
No more blames and guilt trips
It is to set up healthy boundaries
Keep desired, allow undesired to strip

Stop plunging in unwanted worries
Allow oneself to remain at ease
To take one's own stand
Self-love ain't selfish

It's to recognize your inner needs
Recognising all your parts
Accept all unaccepted in you
Give yourself, all that is due

Divergence

If you expect a good behavior
Expect the bad too
For not all will behave
The way you want them to

As long as there is need to excel
There will be fear of fail
And if there is a need for love
You are paving hatred trail

As long as there is need of health
There is certainly seed of sickness
And if there is a need for strength
You are calling for weakness

The more you got to ask for peace
There is risk of fight
And more you want to be away from wrong
You are pushing away the right

As long as there is need to live
There exists fear of death
And more you strive away from poor
You are creating a rift from wealth

How intensely do you crave for light
Decides your journey in dark
The more there is seeking of one
The opposite does embark

What must be done
My dear friend
To set yourself free
Is to drop extremes and let it go
In neutral, you just be

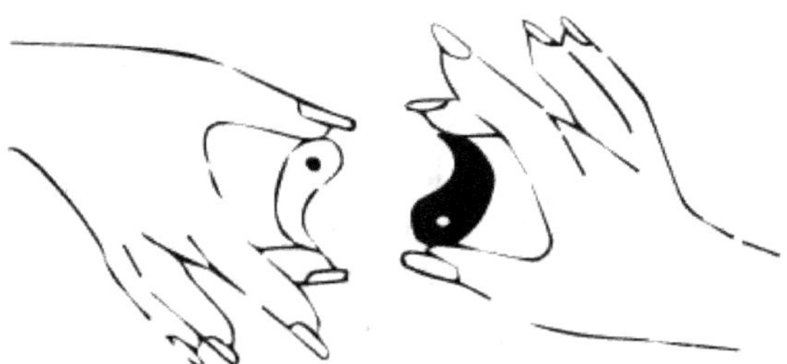

Light

There is still so much need for love
A desire to feel complete
All along, throughout my life
Love is all I seek

No relations is, permanent to identify
All I keep asking is
Who am I?

Staring into the dark starry sky
I ask, how you feel infinite and vast
When I am tiny, awry and dry?

I feel so lonely, incomplete and alone
Dying every moment in my heart
Many times, I feel I am just done

That's when I realize, It's all in Mind
I have the choice to perceive what I want
Dark night or sun shine

All efforts fade, in silence I sit
And the mind fades into heart
Here NOW myself, I meet

The light from formless to taking all forms
Emanating from heart, the light source
Into dust, settles all storm

Dissolving all, nothing remains
Everything just silent and still,
No feelings or emotions, no pleasure or pains

Attention settled in Here and Now
Overflowing all through
Gratitude and love

Silence, stillness and echoing sound
Jumping in joy, my luminous being
Expanding peace, in and around

Recognizing all, shining bright
"I" dissolve in my being
I become Light

Light, just light here and there
I Exist, I am Existence
Always and Everywhere

Running on circumference

Life's running on circumference
From time begin to infinity
Between aversion and affinity

Pain and pleasure come together In one
another's disguise
When tired you are, of this run
Choose to stand and rise

Wake up and walk ahead Travel to the core
Just peace within, no loss no win
Fights with self, no more

Become the center Let the life revolve
Beyond time and space
Witness yourself evolve

You are the Universe You are the core
Not here to run on circumference But for
self-explore

Birth the new

When it's time to birth the new
And it's time to shed the old,
Emerges your deepest dark
It is ok to sit in your vulnerable place, no hurry
to unfold!

When life's falling apart
And nothing helps you cope
Be sure, it's time to rise
just sit in total hope

It's time when you feel so lost
You witness your patterns die
Watch your controls and resistance fall
In a compassionate cry

Sit aloof and tired
The emotions just follow
Allow the purging out
Making space for still and flow

Reflect! what needs to be done
To allow the process unfold
It's natural and sacred too
Let go off all control

If there is any lesson that we ought to learn
Is to surrender it all
Trust, someone's taking care
Won't ever let you fall

And who said it's easy
To chase your brightest light
It would take all your faith
To pass through the darkest night

Anything Real?

In this ever-changing world
Is there anything real?
Extreme polarities, Divergent dual

Pleasure pain, Insanity and sane
Dark night and bright light
Peace or fight

Rich or poor, Sorrow and joy
What do I choose, laughter or cry?

Or do I truly have a choice?
Or just being here to pay the price

What do I look for, what do I seek?
Sometimes strong and sometimes weak

Lost and found Or found and lost
Life is swinging between benefit and cost

What's real and what is fake?
Somebody tell me, for God's sake

Not Good Enough

What I do
When feeling Not good enough
Either just shut down or treat myself tough
Just to prove all my worth
I bounce between sky and earth

Swinging between extremes
Suppressing all tears and screams
The attention is to become the best
Just leaving behind the rest

The other side is to pull myself down
Blame myself for every flaw in town
The attention now is to not be seen
Hide myself behind the scene

I feel tired bouncing between the two
Is there a solution to this, any clue?
How do I walk this distance
When torn apart, finding my existence?

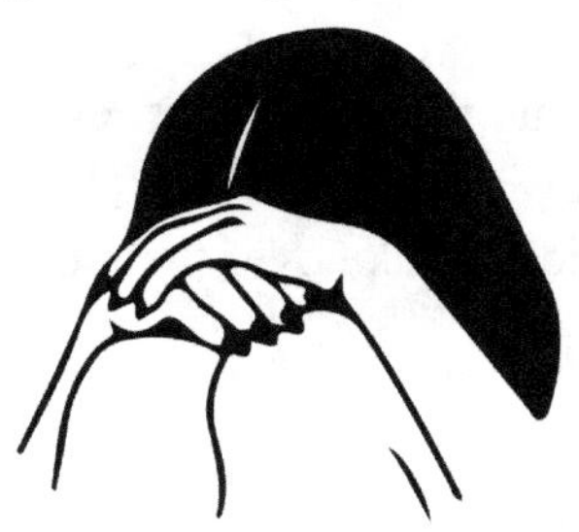

Self-Apology

I deserve an apology from me
For times I tore myself apart
When I neglected my needs
Not listening to my heart

For times of self-sabotage
When I let myself down
The times when I apologized for being myself
Masking like a clown

I forgive myself
For choosing wrong
When I felt vulnerable
But put a face of strong

And for times when I failed to realize
Some battles aren't for me to fight
Sometimes it's just wait and watch
Not proving wrong or right

I forgive myself
For judging me through others' eyes
Dictating how others view me
Allowing vicious take over the wise

Love, care, compassion for self
I choose this, to start anew
And all those beautiful things
Freedom from judgements and views

Choice

It's when I realized that every moment offers a
choice
A choice to live Life
Not remaining stuck in Mind matrix
Stepping out of strife

It's when I realized that I am heading back home
With everyone, who lets go of me
Every string now opens up,
Is setting myself free

And someone's lack of love for me
Is their own truth
And their own seeds of lack,
Is bearing back the fruit

And when I am rejected
Not I feel most bad
It's when I reject myself
The feeling is most sad

Not when others upset me
And I feel let down
I have to not upset me anymore
Comes the glimpse profound

When I am a stranger to myself
It's then I feel alone
Just cannot find peace in others
When need is to find my Own

I must accept myself first
In order to find joy
I must first find peace within
Free from lament and cry

Not every race is worth running
Seldom sit in solitude
Not every experience is worth pursuing
Just remain in gratitude

The only choice is to choose myself
Over all the hurdles and odds
The choice to choose all of love
Stand for self, in all regards

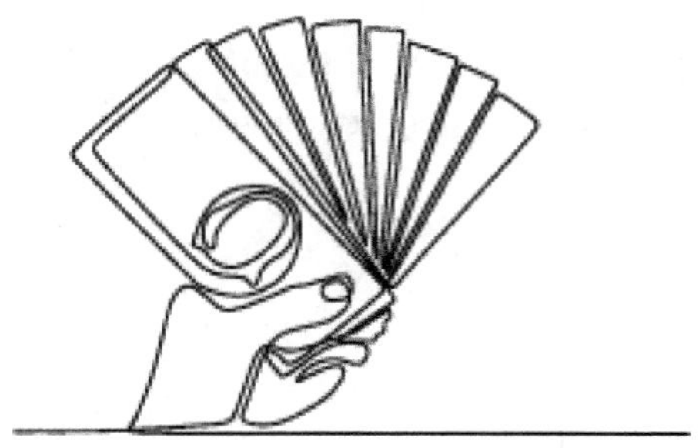

Time is Now..

Feeling joy, live in peace
Every moment choosing this
In Divine plan, accept it all
It bestows run or asks to crawl

Rejoice both pleasure and pain
Bright sunshine or heavy rain
Every moment, remain present
Hearty laugh or woeful lament

Every drama will come to an end
All karma is set to mend
When every doubt comes to rest
Trust! All happens for the Best

Every single breath now felt
All identities are to melt
Every illusion must now dissolve
The Time now has come to evolve

Everyone Needs!

Everyone needs
     love to survive
     love to thrive
     to blossom and fly
     to touch the sky
Everyone needs
     the care, when they cry
     the affection, in times of try
     a lift when falling down
     just a friend when no one's around
Everyone needs
     a pat on the back
     a little support in times of lack
     some presence when feeling void
     some attention of person beside
Everyone needs!

Here and Now!

As I look back
>The journey I recall
How I stood up
>After every fall

The journey of
>Falling from sky
Facing my fears
>Mountain high

From anxiety, panic attacks,
>anger and fear
To now this moment,
>When I am Here!

The emotions came
>just to help
So that I find
>my path to my-self

As I settle
>In this moment now
Everything fades
>Ifs, buts, when, how

The journey was
        To pick all, bits and part
Returning home
        Settling mind in heart

Here, in Now
        Every moment is new
All has ended
        Nothing's due

I can be a mentor too..

It's time to face my biggest fear
How do I move out when death is near

I don't want to die with so much pain
That would leave this life in vain

What if I can choose emotions at the moment of
death
I can come back with a better fate

Too many emotions happening at once
In my mind's eye, a thousand lifetimes run

The saboteur now screamed with a loud cry
I want to live, I don't want to die

And I notice I am not afraid to die
What's driving the show is upon return, how will
be I

I am afraid of pain and sufferings
The lessons in the next life, events and things

The real fear is who will pull my rope
When I sit in distress, with absolute no hope

I may not have the mentors or Guru
Then in next life, now as I do

Spoke a voice, loud and clear
It's all taken care of, Nothing to fear

Every time you get a new try
A part of old is about to die

Watch yourself Now Here, look into you
And I found, I can be a mentor too

I realized I have died many such deaths
The old one dies with every new breath

It's an inevitable part of life cycle
I choose to settle myself in neutral

I rely on me, I can be my guide
The fear dissolved, in ME I confide

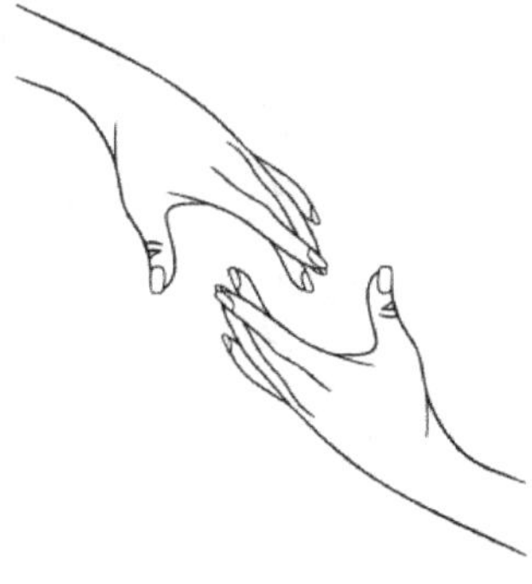

Neutral

Love is showering in many ways
Be open to receive it, anyways

Do not bind to an experience
Feel it fully, until it's done

The Mind, when comes to still
Feelings, emotions now gets to nil

The idea is, to come to neutral
Until you become One, remains no dual

Into the light, going beyond
In union with love and Divine sound

Self-acceptance

The need to be happy
Is where unhappiness resides
When open yourself to unhappiness
In your true being you rejoice

The chase to be somewhere
Is where your mind divides
Being present here and now
It's where duality unites

The presence contains no demands
It's the ocean, loving all its waves
Everything, in-between
It totally dissolves

Every breath is sacred in self
Be it in or out
One is not complete without another
Be it trust or doubts

It's ok to have an unhappy day
In your sadness and gloom
Just get to its roots
No need to mask away

When you find your authentic self
In deep surrender of life
Your inner child falls into your arms
Life is no more a strife

The child can cry, weep or sing
Show the tantrums and rage
As you permit to be what you are
Life gets safe, no more a cage

So, what you seek, outside of you
Is for you to provide for self
Giving permission to every child in you
Standing tall for own help

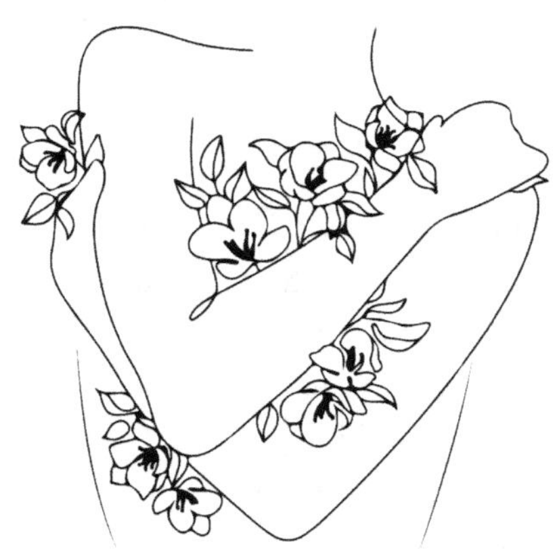

How can I be free?

When I laid back
I felt I was shy
And when I led in front
I felt my pride

When I had no ambitions
I felt I was sad
When I shared my aims
I felt I was mad

When I share advice
I question my guidance
A part of me
Always needs evidence

I questioned my being
Why can't I be at ease
Whatever I do,
I am never at peace

I wanted to share,
I saw, closed ears
So, I embraced myself
And all my fears

I sat at the window
Staring at the mountain and trees
I heard myself whisper
How can I be free?

I sway often,
Between two extremes
Confusing it all
Reality or dreams

I looked at the sky
And asked for clearance
For I knew not
How long this penance

Though, I had known
It's me, who punishes myself
And then a part of me
Is asking, me for help

The sky went still
And there was no breeze
Frozen in the moment
I learnt to unfreeze

The memories, the mind
The emotions are seed
Just in the moment,
I must breathe

For, when in the moment
The mind dissolves
No past, no future
Just Presence evolves